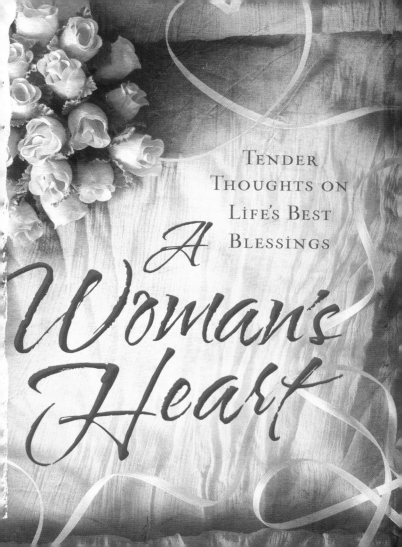

TENDER
THOUGHTS ON
LIFE'S BEST
BLESSINGS

*A Woman's Heart*

© 2012 by Barbour Publishing, Inc.

Written and compiled by Ellyn Sanna.

Print ISBN 978-1-61626-864-0

eBook Editions:
Adobe Digital Edition (.epub) 978-1-62029-052-1
Kindle and MobiPocket Edition (.prc) 978-1-62029-053-8

Cover and interior design: Kirk DouPonce, DogEared Design

Published by Barbour Publishing, Inc., P.O. Box 719, Uhrichsville, Ohio 44683, www.barbourbooks.com

*Our mission is to publish and distribute inspirational products offering exceptional value and biblical encouragement to the masses.*

 Member of the
Evangelical Christian
Publishers Association

Printed in India.

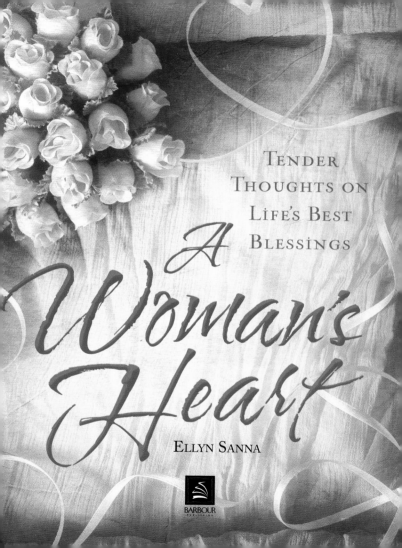

TENDER
THOUGHTS ON
LIFE'S BEST
BLESSINGS

*A Woman's Heart*

Ellyn Sanna

BARBOUR
PUBLISHING

# Contents

# Introduction

As women, we often connect more to our hearts, while the men in our lives may focus more on their brains. But that doesn't mean we women are weak or sentimental!

The word *courage* comes from the Latin word for *heart*—and courage is born in the heart; courageous acts come from the heart. In other words, our tenderness is what makes us strong. It is what allows us to see God's best blessings of joy, love, grace, peace, and hope—and it is what enables us to pass those blessings on to others. We are women of strength and courage because we are also women of heart.

# The Sunny Side
## of Life

*Light is sweet, and it pleases the eyes to see the sun.*
*However many years anyone may live,*
*let him enjoy them all.*

ECCLESIASTES 11:7–8 NIV

# Make Time for Sunshine

Sometimes it seems that our lives are nothing but gray days. From small frustrations to major crises, life can be so *hard*. We get so used to clouds and gloom that sunshine seems like something we'll never experience again. With all the responsibilities and troubles in life, we may feel as though we'd be immature and shallow to even dream of sunny days. Sunshine is for kids, we think; grown-up life is *serious*.

God is there with us in our shadows, of course—but He also made the sunshine, and He wants to share it with us. He wants us to remember that even the dreariest, darkest winters yield way to spring. And when the sun comes out, He doesn't want us to miss it! He calls us to come outside, to play, to laugh, to have a child's heart again.

So don't sit inside your dark house with the windows shut, brooding over life's troubles. And don't be so busy with your grown-up, indoor life that you miss the coming of spring outdoors. If you look outside, you may be surprised to find the sun is actually shining after all. Every now and then, remind yourself to take a break from your life's load—and make time for sunshine. Feel the warmth on your face. Soak up the sense of well-being it brings.

The sunny side of life is every bit as real and valuable as life's gray days. And our God has things He longs to share with you in the sunshine. He wants you to know the reality of His joy and taste the delight of His presence. He wants to see you smile!

There is no duty we so much underrate as the duty of being happy. By being happy we sow anonymous benefits upon the world.

ROBERT LOUIS STEVENSON

Our chief end is to glorify God and to enjoy Him forever.

PRESBYTERIAN CATECHISM

To be a joy-bearer and a joy-giver says everything, for in our life, if one is joyful, it means that one is faithfully living for God, and that nothing else counts; and if one gives joy to others one is doing God's work; with joy without and joy within, all is well.

JANET ERSKINE STUART

*You make known to me the path of life;*
*you will fill me with joy in your presence,*
*with eternal pleasures at your right hand.*

PSALM 16:11 NIV


*The LORD is my strength and my shield; my heart*
*trusts in him, and he helps me. My heart leaps*
*for joy, and with my song I praise him.*

PSALM 28:7 NIV

*Worship the LORD with gladness.*
*Come before him, singing with joy.*

PSALM 100:2 NLT

# A Call to Worship

Where did we ever get the idea that religion was a serious, somber affair? The Bible is full of happy words like *gladness, pleasure, song, praise, joy,* and *rejoice.* Nowhere does it tell us, *Frown. . .sigh. . .disapprove. . .worry. . .be sad . . .think about nothing but sin and sadness and death.*

That is definitely not what the scripture says! And yet that's how some of us act. We don't take seriously God's Word that tells us to be joyful. We often don't even understand what it really means to experience joy.

The Bible's joy is always connected to the presence of God. It is the natural state in which we find ourselves if we walk with

Him. It is the organic by-product of worship. Worship and joy just naturally go together.

The word *worship* is one we may connect to singing praise songs or lifting our hearts in silent adoration to God, and those activities may certainly be aspects of worship. Some days, though, we just don't feel like singing choruses—or the world is too loud for us to find those quiet moments of adoration.

But the Old English root word for worship points us in a slightly different direction and offers us a new perspective. *Worth-ship* was the English word used a thousand-some years ago, and it was based on a two-way relationship between a lord and his servant. The servant's "worth-ship" of the lord gave worth—valor, strength, and value—to the servant as well as the lord, for the two were linked together in a mutual commitment of honor and esteem.

Worship from this perspective is simply the daily living out of a mutual commitment. We can express that commitment in all sorts of ways—from praise choruses to vocal prayer to total silence—but ultimately, it is simply the relationship itself that creates this two-way stream of love and honor. When we enter into this relationship with the Lord of the universe, we receive infinite, eternal value and strength. No wonder worship fills our hearts with joy!

And when we make this daily worship the "serious" focus of our everyday lives, how can we help but sing with joy. . .leap with gladness. . .and rejoice in each and every day?

$\mathcal{L}$ord, teach me to make worship my constant practice. May Your heart and mine be always united in a constant two-way stream of love. Let my entire life—the daily chores, the countless interactions with others, the responsibilities of home and work, the moments of rest—all give You worship. Be at the center of it all. And I know that only then will I truly know Your joy!

*For, lo, the winter is past, the rain is over
and gone; the flowers appear on the earth;
the time of the singing of birds is come.*

SONG OF SOLOMON 2:11–12 KJV


*Rejoice in the Lord always:
and again I say, Rejoice.*

PHILIPPIANS 4:4 KJV

*This is the day which the L*ORD *hath made;*
*we will rejoice and be glad in it.*

PSALM 118:24 KJV

# Never Grow Old

The world tells us that taking time for pleasure, laughter, and play is irresponsible. It insists that we have to be *productive* in some way—every minute that we're awake. With so much we're responsible for, so much we have to accomplish each and every day, we don't have time for the sort of joy that children take for granted. The days just aren't long enough, we tell ourselves. No matter how much we rush, no matter how busy we are, no matter how frantically we hurry from one task to another, we can never get caught up. And meanwhile, the years keep going by, and we keep getting older and older.

But it's not the years that make us old. Instead, we get old when responsibilities loom larger than joys, when we lose our sense of humor, when we forget how to play. We're too busy for such foolishness. . .and our hearts begin to wrinkle and our spiritual shoulders stoop. The sun goes behind the clouds, and everywhere we look we see only shades of gray.

We can choose to live our lives differently. As Christ's followers, we can refuse to grow old. Instead, we can seek out the delight life has to offer, even in the midst of pain and trouble. We can take time to laugh, to play, to rejoice in all God has given us. And when we do, our joy will spread to others.

A child throwing coins into a fountain doesn't care if she's wasting money. She only knows she's having fun—and by doing so she spreads her joy. We can be the same with life's pleasures. We don't have to worry about wasting time. Time is one of God's gifts to us, and we don't need to be afraid to spend it. Instead, we can make room in our lives for delight. We can take time to sit in the sun. . .and simply *be*.

*Where others see but the dawn coming over the hill, I see the soul of God shouting for joy.*

WILLIAM BLAKE

*Be merry, really merry. The life of a true Christian should be a perpetual jubilee, a prelude to the festivals of eternity.*

THEOPHANE VENARD

*The real joy of life is in its play. Play is anything we do for the joy and love of doing it, apart from any profit, compulsion, or sense of duty. It is the real living of life.*

WALTER RAUSCHENBUSCH

$\mathcal{L}$ord, play with me today. Hold my hand
as I go about my tasks—and give me a
poke if I get too busy to laugh. Remind
me to sing. Help me remember to smile.
Put a skip in my step. Tickle my funny bone.
Nudge me whenever I'm missing out
on the sunshine of Your love.

*All the great blessings of my life*
*are present in my thoughts today.*

PHOEBE CARY


*May your life become one of glad and unending*
*praise to the Lord as you journey through this*
*world, and in the world that is to come!*

TERESA OF AVILA


*Joy. . .is the presence of God.*

SAM STORMS

$\mathcal{L}$ord, help me to live my life
always in Your presence, delighting
in Your blessings, rejoicing in Your love.
May my life be a song of joy.

# Unending Love

*Love never gives up.*

1 CORINTHIANS 13:7 NLT

# Practicing Love

Love may be a spiritual quality—but it's also as down to earth and practical as the air we breathe. As human beings, we need love. In fact, psychologists tell us that love is as necessary to our lives as oxygen. The more connected we are to others and to God, the healthier we will be, both physically and emotionally—and the less connected we are, the more we are at risk.

Our culture tends to believe that love "just happens." If we don't feel enough love in our lives, then we're just not one of the lucky people. But love doesn't work that way.

Psychologist Erich Fromm called love "an act of will." To feel love in our lives, we have to make up our minds to act in loving ways. We have to put our love for God and others into practice. And there are concrete ways we do this. Here are some of them:

- Focus on God and others. Don't obsess about your own concerns. Instead, shift your attention outside yourself. Look at God. Notice the person next to you (whether that's your husband, a friend, a coworker, or a stranger you've met in passing).
- Go out of your way to help someone else. Notice the needs around you—and do

something practical to meet them, even in the smallest of ways.

- Practice looking at things from other perspectives besides your own. This could mean something as simple as imagining yourself in another's shoes. It also means truly listening when another speaks. And it means allowing yourself to absorb God's perspective through scripture and prayer.

God's love is never ending. There is nothing we need to do to deserve that love or to draw it to us. But there *are* ways that we can allow that love to flow through us to the world around us.

For [God] is, indeed, a wonderful Father
who longs to pour out His mercy upon us,
and whose majesty is so great that He can
transform us from deep within.

TERESA OF AVILA


Love is an act of endless forgiveness.

JEAN VANIER


When God calls [someone], He does not
repent of it. God does not, as many friends do,
love one day, and hate another. . . . Acts of
grace cannot be reversed. God blots out His
people's sins, but not their names.

THOMAS WATSON

*Love. . .never loses faith, is always hopeful,*
*and endures through every circumstance.*

1 Corinthians 13:7 NLT


*It is of the LORD's mercies that we are not*
*consumed, because his compassions fail not. They*
*are new every morning: great is thy faithfulness.*

Lamentations 3:22–23 KJV


*See what great love the Father has lavished on us,*
*that we should be called children of God!*
*And that is what we are!*

1 John 3:1 NIV

*Love is patient, love is kind. It does not envy, it does not boast, it is not proud. It does not dishonor others, it is not self-seeking, it is not easily angered, it keeps no record of wrongs. Love does not delight in evil but rejoices with the truth. It always protects, always trusts, always hopes, always perseveres. Love never fails. But where there are prophecies, they will cease; where there are tongues, they will be stilled; where there is knowledge, it will pass away.*

1 CORINTHIANS 13:4–8 NIV

# Love's Ingredients

In his first letter to the Corinthians, the apostle Paul spelled out a practical definition of love. These are the fourteen "ingredients" in love's recipe:

1. *Love is patient.* It answers the thousandth question from a toddler; it picks up the dirty socks a spouse always leaves in the middle of the floor; it holds its tongue instead of snapping in anger.
2. *Love is kind.* It doesn't insult others; it is gentle to others' weaknesses; it goes out of its way to do something nice for another.
3. *Love does not envy.* It doesn't begrudge another's good fortune; it doesn't long to possess others' belongings; it rejoices in others' blessings.

4. *Love does not boast.* It doesn't try to impress others; it doesn't brag about its own accomplishments; it doesn't try to inflate its own worth by exaggerating achievements and possessions.
5. *Love is not proud.* It is never arrogant; instead, it is always humble, always willing to be set aside or to take a lower position.
6. *Love does not dishonor others.* It isn't inconsiderate of others' feelings; it pays attentions to others' wishes.
7. *Love is not self-seeking.* It doesn't put self first, but instead sets self to one side.
8. *Love is not easily angered.* It isn't touchy or irritable; it doesn't have a short fuse.
9. *Love keeps no record of wrongs.* It doesn't harp back over and over to something that happened long ago; it doesn't bring up the same list of grievances every time there's a conflict with another.

10. *Love does not delight in evil but it rejoices in truth*. It's never glad when others do wrong or bad things happen to others; it does not gloat or gossip.
11. *Love always trusts, and believes all things*. It gives others the benefit of the doubt; it is loyal; it gives others a second (and third and fourth) chance.
12. *Love always hopes*. It always looks toward the future; it believes that others are capable of living out their fullest potentials.
13. *Love always perseveres*. It doesn't give up on others; it endures through the hard times.
14. *Love never fails*. It is eternal, unending, unlimited, and unconditional.

This list is not only a description of love. It is also a description of God—who *is* love!

$\mathcal{L}$ord, help me to love like You do.
You know I can't do it without Your help.
But with You I can do anything! So please,
Lord, love those around me, through me,
with Your perfect love.

*For great is your love toward me. . . . You, Lord, are a compassionate and gracious God, slow to anger, abounding in love and faithfulness.*

PSALM 86:13, 15 NIV


*The LORD will work out his plans for my life— for your faithful love, O LORD, endures forever. Don't abandon me, for you made me.*

PSALM 138:8 NLT


*For the LORD is good. His unfailing love continues forever, and his faithfulness continues to each generation.*

PSALM 100:5 NLT


*"I have loved you with an everlasting love; I have drawn you with unfailing kindness."*

JEREMIAH 31:3 NIV

*No one has ever seen God. But if we love each other, God lives in us, and his love is brought to full expression in us.*

1 JOHN 4:12 NLT

# Making Love Visible

"Seeing is believing," we often say. It's hard to believe in something we can't see. As human beings, most of us (those of us who have vision) depend on our eyes to understand the world around us. We've all heard the saying, "A picture is worth a thousand words," and the advertising world knows the power of visual images to influence our minds. So do teachers. Abstract concepts are difficult to wrap our minds around—but if we can see something, it instantly becomes easier for us to grasp.

As John points out, none of us have seen God. We know we are told to walk by faith rather than sight (2 Corinthians 5:7)—and yet all of us, at one time or another, have doubted God's love. In a world where terrible things happen, we can't help but wonder if God's love is real. Is God even real? It's hard to believe in something we've never seen. We need a visual image to convince us.

Jesus was that visual image, of course. But now, as His followers, we are called to carry out His work on earth. He wants us each to be a visible embodiment of divine love. Our love makes the invisible God visible. When we act in love toward those around us, demonstrating selflessness and service, others can see God.

Through us, love becomes visible. We are the expression of God to the world.

*Our sweetest experiences of affection are
meant to point us to that realm which is
the real and endless home of the heart.*

HENRY WARD BEECHER

*This is the miracle that happens every
time to those who really love: the more
they give, the more they possess.*

RAINER MARIA RILKE

*The cross is the ultimate evidence that there
is no length the love of God will refuse
to go in effecting reconciliation.*

R. KENT HUGHES

Jesus, make me a portrait of Your love.
Use my hands, my feet, my words, my smile to
show others that You are real. Remind me that
I am here on this earth to carry out Your work
of love. Be visible through me, I pray.

# The Gift of Grace

*For the grace of God has been revealed,
bringing salvation to all people.*

TITUS 2:11 NLT

# New Testament Grace

When we read the word *grace* in our English New Testament, it's translating a Greek word, *charis*. This word was connected to rejoicing; it also implied sweetness, loveliness, favor, goodwill, and kindness. The word occurs in the New Testament Greek at least 170 times!

Our English versions have sometimes translated the same word in different ways, all of which help us to get a fuller picture of what grace looks like. In some places, it has to do with gratitude and thanks. (This is why we "say grace" before a meal.) In other translations, it comes to us as "bounty," "liberality," or "generosity." Sometimes it seems like a joyful, sweet *feeling* we experience; sometimes it appears to be more like an *act* of mercy and love; other times, it appears to be a word that describes a *quality* of utter loveliness; and still others, it looks like something that is given, an undeserved *gift*. And the Greek word has one more shade of meaning that doesn't often come through in English: it has to do with God reaching toward us, a sense of God stretching across the distance between Himself and us, a divine act of leaning forward in eager love.

All these shades of meaning blend

together in our minds, of course. Ultimately, grace takes many forms—but it is always something beautiful God holds out to us in His outstretched arms, leaning to-ward us to give us that which we don't deserve. He gives to us so freely and in such bounty that He fills our entire being with gratitude and joy—and we are saved, made whole forever.

*Grace is no stationary thing, it is ever becoming.
It is flowing straight out of God's heart. Grace
does nothing but re-form and convey God. Grace
makes the soul conformable to the will of God.
God, the ground of the soul, and grace go together.*

MEISTER ECKHART


*The Lord's chief desire is to reveal Himself
to you and, in order for Him to do that,
He gives you abundant grace.*

MADAME JEANNE GUYON


*With each year, we grow in our ability to receive
the endless bounty of grace that God waits to give
us. Grace is like a flower that unfolds a little more
and then a little more. Each day we see more
deeply into the blossom of God's unending creation.*

ALYSON JAMES

*Let us therefore come boldly unto the
throne of grace, that we may obtain mercy,
and find grace to help in time of need.*

HEBREWS 4:16 KJV


*"Because of his grace he declared us
righteous and gave us confidence
that we will inherit eternal life."*

TITUS 3:7 NLT

*But by the grace of God I am what I am: and his grace which was bestowed upon me was not in vain; but I laboured more abundantly than they all: yet not I, but the grace of God which was with me.*

1 CORINTHIANS 15:10 KJV

# Active Grace

In the Old Testament Hebrew Bible, the word translated as *grace* was *chanan*. Like the Greek term, this also had to do with loveliness, but more often it implied favor, an act of blessing. Old Testament grace was not something abstract and hazy; it was something active working in the world.

In both the Old and New Testaments, grace is something that connects God's heart and ours. In the New Testament, however, the sense of inner grace was added to the Old Testament's concept of outward acts of grace. This inner grace is also active, and it is powerful; it changes our hearts. It is something that labored in the apostle Paul's life; it made him who he was, and it allowed him to accomplish great things. The New Testament also tells us that grace is something that makes us strong enough to face the challenges of our days (2 Corinthians 12:9). It is the Spirit of God present in our lives (Hebrews 10:29).

If we have eyes to see, we'll find God's grace everywhere we turn. Grace shines in the sunlight; it touches our lives through a neighbor's smile or a child's laughter; it warms our hearts in acts of unexpected kindness from a passing stranger. And we also find it inside our own hearts. It is the capacity to be kind when we thought we'd used up all our patience; it is the strength we find inside ourselves to make a change for the good; it is our ability to love someone who has hurt us.

Always, God's grace is something that is freely given. There is nothing we can do to earn it. It just shows up in our lives, undeserved.

Oh Lord, how absolutely necessary Your
grace is for me! Without Your grace I
could neither begin anything worthwhile
nor stick with it until it was accomplished—
but because of grace, I can do all things.
Your grace makes me strong. Amen.

*What do you have that God hasn't given you?*
*And if everything you have is from God,*
*why boast as though it were not a gift?*

1 Corinthians 4:7 nlt


*In [Jesus] we have redemption through his blood,*
*the forgiveness of sins, in accordance with the*
*riches of God's grace that he lavished on us.*

Ephesians 1:7–8 niv


*So the Word became human and made his home*
*among us. He was full of unfailing love and*
*faithfulness. . . . From his abundance we have all*
*received one gracious blessing after another.*

John 1:14, 16 nlt

*For by grace are ye saved through faith;*
*and that not of yourselves: it is the gift of God.*

EPHESIANS 2:8 KJV

# Free Grace

We live in a world where you can't get something for nothing. Everything comes back to: "You scratch my back, I'll scratch yours." We learned the principle when we were very young, on the playground maybe, when some little boy or girl said, "You give me your marbles, and I'll give you my jump rope." When we grew up, we understood that we wouldn't get far in life—or make any money— if we didn't work hard. Nice clothes and cars and houses—all the good things this world has to offer—cost money, and most of us can only get money if we work for it. We have to earn it.

We tend to carry this hard-won wisdom into our relationship with God. We assume He works from the same principles—that we'll have to earn His favor. We think God will only give to us if we give to Him. So we try to "be good." We work hard to look like Christians on the outside. We follow all the rules. It's never good enough, of course. No matter how hard we try, we can never make ourselves good.

And it doesn't matter! God turns our human rules upside down. He gives to us when we do absolutely nothing. He gives to us when we don't deserve anything. He gives to us no matter what. Christ's life and death are the embodiment of God's giving nature, His commitment to give absolutely everything to us humans, no matter how broken we may be. That's grace.

Grace asks nothing of us except trust. It asks us to let go of our own efforts so that grace can work through us. When we open our hearts, grace flows into us. And God's grace within us then flows out of us, as well, changing the world around us.

*There is nothing but God's grace. We walk upon it; we breathe it; we live and die by it; it makes the nails and axles of the universe.*

ROBERT LOUIS STEVENSON

*To me, every hour of the day and night is an unspeakably perfect miracle.*

WALT WHITMAN

Lord, let me simply let go and trust You. Teach me to see Your grace written in the lines of my life. Remind me that Your grace surrounds me, everywhere I turn. Let me find Your peace as I let myself rest in grace. Amen.

*All men who live with any degree of
serenity live by some assurance of grace.*

REINHOLD NIEBUHR


*I do not at all understand the mystery of grace—
only that it meets us where we are but does
not leave us where it found us.*

ANNE LAMOTT


*Grace is the ability to live once more like a child,
delighting in the passage of time, with no fear for
the future. Grace is the amazing good news that
because of Jesus, we truly live in a world where we
need not be bothered by death's looming shadow.*

ALYSON JAMES

Lord, thank You for all the undeserved gifts You have given to me so generously. Thank You that I can do nothing to earn Your love, that You simply give it to me, freely and eagerly, because that's Your very nature! Amen.

Unexpected
Blessings

*From his abundance we have all received*
*one gracious blessing after another.*

JOHN 1:16 NLT

# God's Surprise Packages

Some people only exist. They go through their days with their eyes on the ground, plodding along as though life were an endurance test.

We need to learn to look up or we'll miss many of the good things God longs for us to have. We'll overlook the small joys and tiny blessings God has showered into our lives.

But sometimes we're so focused on the big things—finances, our health, our loved ones' well-being—that we forget to notice the many small ways God shows His love. Each new sunrise, each good meal, each warm bath or good night's sleep, all send us love messages from our Father.

A blessing can be something as simple as:

- A phone call to a special friend.
- Lunch at a favorite restaurant with someone you love.
- A book you've been wanting to read.
- Time alone to savor something special.
- A cup of tea or coffee or a tall, cool drink.
- A walk through nature.
- A hot bath.
- An e-mail that makes you smile.

Cultivate the attitude that each day that comes is a brand-new present from God to be unwrapped with joy. Hold out your hands. Don't be afraid to open His packages of blessings.

*Open wide the windows of our spirits and fill
us full of light; open wide the door of our hearts,
that we may receive and entertain Thee with
all our powers of adoration.*

CHRISTINA ROSSETTI


*Let there be many windows in your soul, that all
the glory of the universe may beautify it.*

ELLA WHEELER WILCOX


*The soul should always stand ajar,
ready to welcome the ecstatic experience.*

EMILY DICKINSON

Give freely and become more wealthy;
be stingy and lose everything. The generous
will prosper; those who refresh others
will themselves be refreshed.

PROVERBS 11:24–25 NLT


Then Jesus turned to his disciples and said,
"God blesses you who are poor, for the Kingdom
of God is yours. God blesses you who are hungry
now, for you will be satisfied. God blesses you who
weep now, for in due time you will laugh. What
blessings await you when people hate you and
exclude you and mock you and curse you as evil
because you follow the Son of Man. When that
happens, be happy! Yes, leap for joy! For a great
reward awaits you in heaven."

LUKE 6:20–23 NLT

*Faith is the confidence that what we hope for will actually happen; it gives us assurance about things we cannot see.*

HEBREWS 11:1 NLT

# Blessings Still on Their Way

Sometimes we're so focused on the blessings we *don't* have yet, that it's hard to be thankful for the blessings we already have. Like children, we hate to wait. We get impatient, and we forget that God sees from a perspective outside time. He knows that He plans to give us everything we need at exactly the right moment. While we wait on His timing, we need to cultivate a grateful heart for both the things that we have—and the things for which we are still waiting.

In the Old Testament, the Lord commanded Israel to count their harvest, beginning the day after the Sabbath during Passover (Leviticus 23:15). For nearly two thousand years, the Jewish people had no homeland, and they had no harvest to count—and yet they continued to obey this Old Testament commandment. They counted a harvest that from the world's perspective simply didn't exist. But they counted it as an act of faith, a visible demonstration of their faith in God.

In the New Testament, we're told that faith is the conviction of things not seen. This means we can begin to give thanks for

blessings we have yet to receive. Like the
Jewish people, we can count on a harvest that's
yet to come. Whether it's guidance to know
the right choice for our lives, healing for a
wounded relationship or an ill loved
one, or the answer to a painful problem,
we can be grateful for the blessing that waits
to be revealed. We don't know *how* God will
bless us, but we know He *will*. All we have to
do is be patient—and wait to see the unexpected blessings He will pour into our lives.

$\mathcal{L}$ord Jesus, I thank You for the many, many blessings You have given to me in the past. I thank You for all the blessings You are giving me now, at this very moment. And I thank You for the countless blessings You still have in store for me in the future. Amen.

"Today I have given you the choice between life and death, between blessings and curses. Now I call on heaven and earth to witness the choice you make. Oh, that you would choose life!"

DEUTERONOMY 30:19 NLT

LORD, you alone are my inheritance,
my cup of blessing.

PSALM 16:5 NLT

But those who live to please the Spirit will
harvest everlasting life from the Spirit.
So let's not get tired of doing what is good.
At just the right time we will reap a harvest
of blessing if we don't give up.

GALATIANS 6:8–9 NLT

*And God will generously provide all you need.*
*Then you will always have everything you need*
*and plenty left over to share with others.*

2 CORINTHIANS 9:8 NLT

# Count Your Blessings

How often do you take time to reflect on the blessings in your life?

If we're honest, most of us would have to admit that our attention tends to focus on all that is wrong with our lives, instead of all that is right. God deserves our thanks for His many blessings—and to be truly healthy and happy we need to have a grateful heart.

Recently, two psychologists decided to test the value of "counting our blessings." They asked a group of students to respond to a weekly questionnaire for ten weeks. The first group listed five things they were grateful for each week. The second group listed five hassles or problems they'd had in the past week. The final group simply wrote down five "events or circumstances" from the past week.

For the most part, the events listed by all three groups contained small events. No one had any major crises or life-changing events. Some students said they were grateful for "waking up this morning," or "for wonderful parents." Those who reported "hassles" listed things like "hard to find parking," "messy kitchen," or "having a horrible test in health psychology."

Guess what? The students in the "gratitude group" were not only emotionally happier at the end of the ten weeks, but they were also physically healthier. They reported that they had more energy for exercise, they got more sleep, and they felt more rested when they got up.

In other words, when we count our blessings. . .we are blessed! As we say thank You to God, He heaps blessing upon blessing into our lives.

Life is what we are alive to. It is not length but breadth. . . . Be alive to. . .goodness, kindness, purity, love, history, poetry, music, flowers, stars, God, and eternal hope.

MALTBIE D. BABCOCK

Though we travel the world over to find the beautiful, we must carry it with us or we find it not.

RALPH WALDO EMERSON

Into all our lives, in many simple, familiar, homely ways, God infuses this element of joy from the surprises of life, which unexpectedly brighten our days, and fill our eyes with light.

HENRY WADSWORTH
LONGFELLOW

Lord, teach me to see Your blessings. Give me eyes to see all You have done in the world around me. Clear the doubt and gloom from my vision. Let me look up and see Your face; let me reach out and take Your blessings.

Amen.

*The voyage of discovery is not in seeking new landscapes but in having new eyes.*

MARCEL PROUST


*Never lose an opportunity of seeing anything that is beautiful; for beauty is God's handwriting— a wayside sacrament. Welcome it in every fair face, in every fair sky, in every fair flower, and thank God for it as a cup of blessing.*

RALPH WALDO EMERSON


*Whether sixty or sixteen, there is in every human being's heart the love of wonder, the sweet amazement at the stars and star-like things, the undaunted challenge of events, the unfailing childlike appetite for what-next, and the joy of the game of living.*

SAMUEL ULLMAN

Lord of love, give me a childlike vision once again. Let me see Your beauty in the world around me, in children's voices and friends' smiles, in the morning sunlight and the comfort of a warm bed. May I drink deep from Your cup of blessing! Amen.

The Comfort
of Peace

*For unto us a child is born, unto us a son is given. . .*
*and his name shall be called. . . The Prince of Peace.*

ISAIAH 9:6 KJV

# The Prince of Peace

Most of us are familiar with this verse
from the prophet Isaiah as it is sung in
Handel's *Messiah*. We connect the words
with Christmas—the birth of the Christ
Child—and we seldom go much further than
that in our thoughts about the Prince of Peace.
But God wants us to experience Christ's peace
not just as a pretty Christmas message, but in
our ordinary, everyday lives.

The Hebrew word that is translated *peace*
is actually *shalom*. It's a word that is rich with
significance in the Hebrew language, with
many shades of meaning that add greater

depth to our usual concept of peace as simply the absence of conflict. These meanings include completeness, prosperity, safety, contentment, health, rest, comfort, ease, and soundness. What's more, the word that the King James Version of the Bible translated as *prince* is actually a word that's closer to commander, keeper, guardian, or warden. The word *shepherd* comes to mind as well!

In other words, Jesus is the One who guards our lives, bringing peace into them every day. He leads us along paths that will bring us to comfort and contentment. He works to make us whole and healthy. He wants us know that in His presence, we are safe and sound. We can relax, trusting Him to be the

One who brings shalom to us, even on our most stressful days.

Jesus said, " 'I have told you these things, so that in me you may have peace. In this world you will have trouble. But take heart! I have overcome the world'" (John 16:33 NIV). Trust Him to be the guardian of your mind and of your life. Allow Him to create shalom even in the midst of your life's troubles.

*Let my soul take refuge. . .beneath the shadow of Your wings; let my heart, this sea of restless waves, find peace in You, O God.*

AUGUSTINE

*When you have. . .accomplished your daily task, go to sleep in peace. God is awake.*

VICTOR HUGO

*And if tonight my soul may find her peace in sleep, and sink in good oblivion, and in the morning wake like a new-opened flower, then I have been dipped again in God, and new-created.*

D. H. LAWRENCE

*May the God of hope fill you with all joy
and peace as you trust in him, so that
you may overflow with hope.*

ROMANS 15:13 NIV

*The LORD bless thee, and keep thee: The LORD
make his face shine upon thee, and be gracious
unto thee: The LORD lift up his countenance
upon thee, and give thee peace.*

NUMBERS 6:24–26 KJV

*The LORD gives strength to his people;
the LORD blesses his people with peace.*

PSALM 29:11 NIV

*For he himself is our peace, who has made
the two groups one and has destroyed the
barrier, the dividing wall of hostility.*

EPHESIANS 2:14 NIV

# Break Down the Walls!

What disturbs your peace more than anything
else? It may be worries and fears for the future.
Often, though, it's feelings of resentment
against someone who is not treating you
right. You nurse those justified feelings of
indignation. . .and they build inside you,
robbing you of your peace. Even if you and
the other person have decided not to argue
about your disagreement anymore, the wall
of hostility is still there. It's really just a state
of cold war! Nothing has been settled, and
the same old argument is lurking behind the
barriers you've built between you. It's just

waiting for a chance to spill out the next time there's a crack in that wall.

When we find ourselves in a situation like this, it's no wonder we can't feel peace in our hearts! But Paul writes to the Ephesians that there's an answer to this all-too-common situation. The answer is not a technique for conflict resolution. It's a person. It's Jesus Himself.

Our peace with others is disturbed whenever our peace with Jesus is disrupted. When we let down the barriers around our hearts and let Him live inside our hearts, He becomes our peace. He breaks down the walls of hostility within us—the voices that insist on our own way, the selfishness, our need to be in control—and from that state of inner peace and wholeness, we can find new, constructive roads to peace in the relationships that give us trouble. We will find we no longer look at others as separate and opposed to our needs. Instead, we can be truly one.

*D*ear Jesus, be my peace, I pray. I let go of my need to be in control. I give You all my selfishness. Take these ugly gifts—and transform them into something lovely. May I be united once more with those I have separated myself from, just as You and Your Father are one. Even more important, dear Lord, make me one with You! Amen.

*"Be still, and know that I am God."*

PSALM 46:10 NIV


*Cast all your anxiety on him
because he cares for you.*

1 PETER 5:7 NIV


*"My Presence will go with you,
and I will give you rest."*

EXODUS 33:14 NIV


*Those who love your instructions
have great peace and do not stumble.*

PSALM 119:165 NLT

*"God blesses those who are humble,*
*for they will inherit the whole earth."*

MATTHEW 5:5 NLT

# The Peace of Humility

Sometimes, the thing that robs our hearts of peace is our dissatisfaction with who we are. We want to be smarter. . .prettier. . . thinner. . .funnier. We compare ourselves to others around us, and we find that we never seem to measure up. We wish we could accomplish as much as our sister seems to in a day, or that we could keep our homes as tidy as our neighbor does, or that our children would behave as well as our friends' children do. We wish we were better cooks. . .calmer. . .more skillful at our careers. . .more creative. We wish our hair looked better!

When Jesus hears our minds chattering along like this, He probably longs to whisper, "Shush!" As the keeper and guardian of our peace, He asks us to simply take from Him the gift of ourselves. He wants us to humbly accept the people we are—and then offer those people, with all their imperfections, back to Him. He wants us to make peace with ourselves as we are.

What stands in our way when we try to reach out and take this peace from Him? Perhaps it's our pride, our need to be better than others, to impress others, to stand out from the crowd. Somehow, we manage to be both insecure, unsure of our own worth, and selfishly arrogant, all at the same time!

Jesus says to us, however, "The greatest among you must be a servant. But those who exalt themselves will be humbled, and those who humble themselves will be exalted" (Matthew 23:11–12 NLT). In Jesus, we can be truly complete, at peace with ourselves.

*Nothing in all creation is so like God as stillness.*

MEISTER ECKHART


*Let nothing disturb you, let nothing frighten you:*
*everything passes away except God;*
*God alone is sufficient.*

TERESA OF AVILA


*Where the soul is full of peace and joy,*
*outward surroundings and circumstances*
*are of comparatively little account.*

HANNAH WHITALL SMITH


*True silence is the rest of the mind;*
*it is to the spirit what sleep is to the*
*body, nourishment and refreshment.*

WILLIAM PENN

Lord, help me to be at peace with who I am. Let me rest in the knowledge that You love me, just as I am. Teach me to be content in whatever state I find myself. I know that You are all I'll ever need. Amen.

Lasting Friendship

*Dear friends, let us love one another,*
*for love comes from God.*

1 JOHN 4:7 NIV

# Biblical Friendship

In a book called *Life Together*, the German theologian Dietrich Bonhoeffer wrote that human beings cannot be truly alive if they are dependent only on themselves. Each of us needs spiritual nourishment and life—what Bonhoeffer calls the Word—from outside our own boundaries. The Word comes to us daily and anew, says Bonhoeffer, through the mouths of others. As friends, we bring to each other the "divine Word of salvation" in fresh new ways.

Think about it. Our friends are often the ones who keep us from being constantly preoccupied with our own lives, our own troubles and pleasures, and trifling concerns. Left to ourselves, most of us would just spin around inside our own heads, buzzing in tiny circles like bees caught inside a window. Friendship throws open the window and lets those silly bees fly free. It lets in the fresh air and helps us regain a more balanced sense of perspective. Friendship is good for us.

What's more, the Gospel of the New Testament—the Good News of Jesus Christ—is made real through friendship. The faith described by Jesus cannot be lived alone. Friendship is what gives Christ's body strength; our relationships with others are the church's bones and muscles. In these friendships, Christ's life is given flesh once again. We are His hands and feet.

We see God through our friends. God is present in their words and laughter, helping hands and sympathetic tears. He speaks to us through their voices. He loves us through them. And we return that love to our friends. This reciprocal self-giving reflects the Trinity, for Father, Son, and Holy Spirit give themselves to each other, united by a divine friendship. And it's this great, spiritual reality that is made real every time we send an e-mail to a friend. . .pick up the phone to say hello. . . or take time simply to sit and talk!

*Thank you, my friend, for seeing all my faults—
and loving me anyway. Thank you for knowing
the real me—wrinkles and warts—and yet
still helping me to believe I'm beautiful.*

LISA BIANDOLILLO

*A true friend never gets in your way
unless you happen to be going down.*

ARNOLD H. GLASOW

*Silences make the real conversations between
friends. Not the saying but the never
needing to say is what counts.*

MARGARET LEE RUNBECK

*A friend is always loyal.*

PROVERBS 17:17 NLT

*The heartfelt counsel of a friend is
as sweet as perfume and incense.*

PROVERBS 27:9 NLT

*Wounds from a sincere friend are
better than many kisses from an enemy.*

PROVERBS 27:6 NLT

# The Stability of Friendship

Life comes at us so fast that we're often left confused. We need some sort of framework or structure, some way to sort it out into something we can grasp. Otherwise, all the events and circumstances tumble into chaos.

Talking with a friend, sharing our lives, can help us sort through our lives and find that sense of order. After talking with a wise friend, life no longer seems like a jumble of happenstance. A faithful friend's words—even when we don't want to hear them!—can point us toward the eternal meaning that's hidden at life's center.

Women seem to be especially good at sifting through life's random meanings together. We examine the events of each other's lives; we hold up mirrors for each other, allowing friends to understand themselves better. We shine light on who each other is.

Friendship helps us not only recognize our own identities; it also helps us have the strength to claim those identities, to live them out. V. Solovyov, author of *The Meaning of Love*, puts it this way: "Having discerned and loved the truth of another, not in the abstract but in the substance. . .we reveal and make actual our own authentic truth. . .in our capacity to live not only in ourselves but in another." This means that true friendship turns us both inward and outward. In friendship we not only recognize aspects of ourselves, but we also learn to identify with those who are different from ourselves.

Friendship gives our lives stability. It changes the way we think about ourselves as well as the way we look at others. It teaches us new perspectives. It allows us to see with God's eyes.

Thank You, God, for my friends. Thank You for all the ways I see Your face in them. I pray that they may see You in me as well. May our friendship always give You glory. Amen.

*You are better off to have a friend than to be all alone, because then you will get more enjoyment out of what you earn. If you fall, your friend can help you up. But if you fall without having a friend nearby, you are really in trouble.*

ECCLESIASTES 4:9–10 CEV

*"Greater love has no one than this: to lay down one's life for one's friends."*

JOHN 15:13 NIV

"*I no longer call you servants, because a servant does not know his master's business. Instead, I have called you friends, for everything that I learned from my Father I have made known to you.*"

# The Freedom of Friendship

*Merriam-Webster's Dictionary* tells us that our word *friend* comes from Old English roots that meant both "to love" and "to free." That is what friendship does: it ties us together with love even while it sets us free to be uniquely ourselves. "I no longer call you slaves," Jesus told His disciples. "Instead, I have called you friends, people who are dear to Me, people I think of as My equals." In other words, Jesus was not communicating with His disciples as a superior does with his inferiors.

A slave belongs to his master, so of course slave and master cannot be equals. Friends, however, speak openly with each other on equal footing. They trust each other without reserve. They share their plans and goals with each other, and they talk over that which is most important to them. This is the sort of friendship Jesus had with His disciples (and the sort of friendship He wants to have with us as well).

Jesus understood that friendship is squelched by feelings of superiority or possessiveness. Real friends know they don't exist purely for the other's benefit. They respect each other's separate interests. They work to protect and defend each other's rights. They don't try to own or control each other. They don't lord it over each other or try to make the other one feel inferior in some way.

Do we think of our friends as our equals? Or do we ever think of them more as slaves? Christ wants us to love our friends enough to set them free.

*Walking with a friend in the dark is
better than walking alone in the light.*

HELEN KELLER


*A true friend is willing to sit with you in
the dark, to go with you into the silence,
to bear the discomfort and helplessness of
being able to do nothing except be there
at your side in the quiet darkness.*

RACHEL LINDSAY


*A friend who can laugh with you is a wonderful
thing—but a friend who will cry with
you is one who will last forever.*

LISA BIANDOLILLO

Dear Lord, help me to truly want what is best for my friends. Let me never think of them, in even the smallest way, as my slaves! Remind me to see them as they truly are, Your special children, Your amazing creations, and may I always share this perspective with them. Use me in whatever way You can to set them free from anything that holds them back from being all that You want them to be.

*Friendship can mean many things,*
*but ultimately, it means a commitment*
*to the other's well-being.*

JESSIE JESSUP

*A true friend reminds you of the*
*dreams you've forgotten—and insists*
*you give them one more chance.*

ESTHER HOWELL

*Friends. . .cherish each other's hopes.*
*They are kind to each other's dreams.*

HENRY DAVID THOREAU

*I* am so grateful, Lord, for the friends You've given me. I ask that You use my friendships to help me become the person You want me to be. Show me ways to shine Your light into the lives of my friends. We want You to be the center of our relationships. Amen.

# Hope for Tomorrow

*Don't worry about anything;*
*instead, pray about everything.*

PHILIPPIANS 4:6 NLT

# Worry vs. Hope

Not very many of us lie awake at night filled with hope. We're much more likely to lie there consumed with worries! Instead of imaging all the wonderful things God has in store for us, we use our imaginations to picture scenarios of doom and dread. *What if such and such happens,* we think. And then we flesh out exactly what that would look like, first one way and then another. And that "such and such" is never something wonderful and happy. It's always something frightening or sad, something that fills our hearts with anxiety.

As women, most of us seem prone to

mulling things over in our minds. Even Mary, the mother of Jesus, "pondered" the events of Jesus' life in her heart. This pondering and mulling aren't necessarily bad things. New insights can come to us in the process. New awareness of God and others can also come from it. But that's only if we make the process a positive one instead of a negative one. Mulling over fears only makes them loom larger; pondering worries robs our hearts of optimism and hope.

The Bible tells us that prayer is the antidote to worry. When we turn our mulling into prayer, worry can be transformed into hope. But we need to practice using our imaginations in positive ways. Rick Warren wrote, "If you can worry, you can meditate, for worry is negative meditation." It's the focus of our thoughts that makes the difference between a positive meditation and a sleepless night of worry. When we turn our thoughts to God and His promises, our outlook changes. We begin to experience hope instead of worry.

*The future enters into us, in order to transform itself in us, long before it happens.*

RAINER MARIA RILKE

*We walk without fear, full of hope and courage and strength to do His will, waiting for the endless good which He is always giving as fast as He can get us able to take it in.*

GEORGE MACDONALD

*Always be in a state of expectancy, and see that you leave room for God to come in as He likes.*

OSWALD CHAMBERS

*One thing I ask from the LORD, this only do I seek: that I may dwell in the house of the LORD all the days of my life, to gaze on the beauty of the LORD and to seek him in his temple.*

PSALM 27:4 NIV

*No one who hopes in you will ever be put to shame.*

PSALM 25:3 NIV

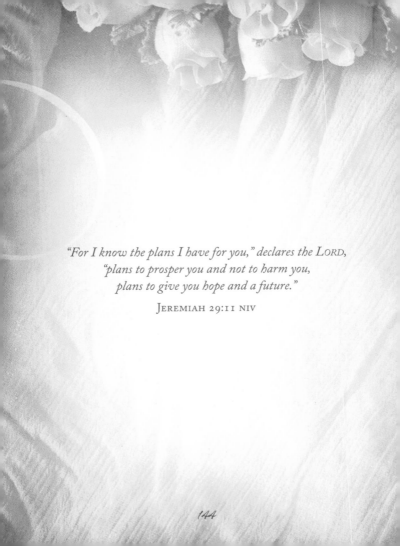

"For I know the plans I have for you," declares the Lord,
"plans to prosper you and not to harm you,
plans to give you hope and a future."

JEREMIAH 29:11 NIV

# Hope for the Future

Sometimes it seems easier to face the future
with fear rather than hope. We feel as though
if we brace ourselves for the worst, we can be
ready for it. But God wants us to be women of
hope, not fear.

It's only natural to fear the unknown, to feel
anxiety as we face the future. Four-year-olds
often fear kindergarten; children sometimes
fear adulthood; and adults fear major life
changes like a move across the country, a new
job, or other new responsibilities. We may fear
old age. And death is the ultimate fear.

When we look back, though, we usually

find that when the change we dreaded actually arrived, we were ready for it—and it brought us greater freedom, greater satisfaction, greater happiness than what we had experienced before. The four-year-old is not ready for kindergarten—but the five-year-old usually is; the eight-year-old is not ready for the responsibilities of adulthood—but the twenty-two-year-old revels in them; and the new job or new home that filled us with anxiety brings with it new friends and new accomplishments that fulfill us in ways we never imagined. Old age has special rewards of its own—and death, that great unknown, will lead us into the presence of God.

Orthodox Jews frequently said this prayer as part of their services: "I believe with perfect faith in the coming of the Messiah; and even though he may tarry, nevertheless, I wait each day for his coming." Despite generations of exile and persecution, they claimed this hope, this state of expectant readiness. As Christians, followers of the Messiah Jesus Christ, we have even more reason to be confident. We can look toward the future with hope and expectation, excited about what God will do for us each and every new day.

Lord, teach me to face the future with hope and confidence. Transform my worries into prayer, and remind me that You have everything under control. Give me hope for all my tomorrows, because You hold them in Your hands. Amen.

"What no eye has seen, what no ear has heard,
and what no human mind has conceived" —
the things God has prepared for those who love him.

1 CORINTHIANS 2:9 NIV


Lead me by your truth and teach me,
for you are the God who saves me.
All day long I put my hope in you.

PSALM 25:5 NLT

*You go before me and follow me. You place your hand of blessing on my head. Such knowledge is too wonderful for me, too great for me to understand!*

PSALM 139:5–6 NLT

# Active Hope

Sometimes hope seems to take more courage than we can muster. There is so much unknown in our lives, so much that seems threatening. Like an animal caught in the headlights of oncoming doom, we stand frozen, staring helplessly ahead, trying to see the path before we dare to take a step. And all the while, life rushes at us through the darkness.

When we finding ourselves terrified, asking, "What should I do? How can I find hope?" the answer is often far simpler than we think. Our hearts are beating with God's love;

we can open them to others. He has entrusted us with gifts and talents; we can use them for His service. He goes before us each step of the way; we can walk through the darkness in faith, one step at a time. We can choose to take action, despite our fears, to venture out into the unknown with the One who knows all.

Sometimes, though, we feel as though we can't make it through one more day. Struggles, stress, and pain are overwhelming. We may cry out (to God, to life), "Please. No more! I can't endure anything else." When that happens, it's hard to find hope.

But ask yourself: Can you make it through the next hour? If so, put your energy into that, no more. If you truly *can't* make it through the

next hour, can you endure the next half hour. . .
the next fifteen minutes. . .the next
minute? Then commit yourself to that
small space of time and look no further
ahead. Take hours, minutes, moments as they
come, one at a time.

Don't run ahead. Do what you can now.
Act in hope for a better tomorrow, even if
you feel as though you're living your life an
inch at a time. And at the end of the day, let
everything drop into God's hands. He already
knows the future, and He's already there,
waiting for you.

Rely on Him to fulfill your hopes in ways
you never could have expected.

*Finish every day and be done with it. You have done what you could. . . . Tomorrow is a new day; begin it well and serenely and with too high a spirit to be cumbered with your old nonsense. This day is all that is good and fair. It is too dear, with its hopes and invitations, to waste a moment on yesterdays.*

RALPH WALDO EMERSON

*Far away, there in the sunshine, are my highest aspirations. . . . I can look up and see their beauty, believe in them, and try to follow where they lead.*

LOUISA MAY ALCOTT

*Hope, you may say, is a bud upon the plant of faith, a bud from the root of faith; the flower is joy and peace.*

GEORGE MACDONALD

God, I ask that You plant in my
heart the root of faith so that my life
may blossom with joy and hope. Amen.

Strength to Endure

*Is any thing too hard for the LORD?*

GENESIS 18:14 KJV

# Limitless Strength

At one time or another, all of us have problems that seem insurmountable. When that happens, maybe we should try spending some time outdoors on a starry night, lying on our backs, looking up at the endless reaches of space. It's a good way to get our perspectives back!

The Bible tells us that even Abraham needed to refer to the starry sky to regain his faith in God. Abraham had an insurmountable problem: he and his wife had no children— and now it looked as though they never would, for they were both getting old. But God told

Abraham to look up at the stars and try to count them; and then He promised Abraham that his children would be as many as the stars. Nothing, God reminded Abraham, is too hard for the Lord.

The next time your circumstances seem too big to handle, make a list of all the things that are overwhelming you. By defining them, they will often seem less overwhelming. Instead of trouble clouding your vision, you may be able to see your difficulties' true dimensions, one at a time.

Once you have your list, go through each item, one by one, and place it in God's hands. Remember, those hands are the ones that created the universe. Our strength has limits—but God's doesn't. He has the power and the creativity to shape your life in amazing ways.

When your own strength fails, that's not necessarily a bad thing! Because now you can rely on God's instead.

God moves in a mysterious way
His wonders to perform;
He plants His footsteps in the sea,
And rides upon the storm.

WILLIAM COWPER


*Our enemies were trying to frighten us and to
keep us from our work. But I asked God to give
me strength. . . . When our enemies in the
surrounding nations learned that the work
was finished, they felt helpless, because they
knew that our God had helped us.*

NEHEMIAH 6:9, 16 CEV

*Then shall we know, if we follow on to know the*
*LORD: his going forth is prepared as the morning;*
*and he shall come unto us as the rain, as the latter*
*and former rain unto the earth.*

HOSEA 6:3 KJV

*And let us run with endurance the race*
*God has set before us. We do this by keeping*
*our eyes on Jesus, the champion who*
*initiates and perfects our faith.*

HEBREWS 12:1–2 NLT

*The LORD will guide you always; he will satisfy*
*your needs in a sun-scorched land. . . .*
*You will be like a well-watered garden,*
*like a spring whose waters never fail.*

ISAIAH 58:11 NIV

*No discipline seems pleasant at the time, but painful.*
*Later on, however, it produces a harvest of righteousness*
*and peace for those who have been trained by it.*

<small>Hebrews 12:11 NIV</small>

# Enduring the Unendurable

Sometimes, life just seems to wear us down. We can usually cope with the endless mini-crises that fill our lives—but eventually, sooner or later, we all reach a point where we want to just throw up our hands and give up. It may be some small event that's the tipping point—or it may be a major life change, an illness or the death of a close friend or loved one. Whatever it is, it's the last straw. Life just doesn't make any sense, and we're at the end of our strength.

God never wants us to feel unnecessary pain, and His heart aches for us when we feel like this. But He also wants us to learn that life was never about our strength. And our ability to makes sense of life never really amounted to much of anything! He longs for us to let go of our need to be in control of our own lives—and finally, totally, trust Him.

Alexander Solzhenitsyn, the Russian author who spent ten years in a Soviet work camp, wrote, "I nourished my soul there, and I say without hesitation: 'Bless you, prison, for having been in my life.'" The prophet Isaiah also learned to see a purpose in the pain he had endured: "Surely it was for my benefit that I suffered such anguish" (38:17 NIV).

When you reach the end of your rope—

you'll find God there, His hand held out. You'll realize then that the silly rope was never all that much use to you anyway, and you'll gladly let it drop so you can take the hand of the One who loves you. When you do, you'll find you have strength to endure what had once seemed unendurable.

When I get to the end of my rope, dear Lord, remind me to take Your hand. Thank You that You have all the strength I'll ever need. Teach me to rely on You instead of on my own abilities. I know that when I do, You'll help me to endure. You'll get me through whatever life throws at me. Amen.

"Ah, Sovereign LORD, you have made the heavens and the earth by your great power and outstretched arm. Nothing is too hard for you."

"Do not fear, for I am with you; do not be dismayed, for I am your God. I will strengthen you and help you; I will uphold you with my righteous right hand."

ISAIAH 41:10 NIV

And I am certain that God, who began the good work within you, will continue his work until it is finally finished on the day when Christ Jesus returns.

PHILIPPIANS 1:6 NLT

"The LORD has forsaken me,
the Lord has forgotten me."

ISAIAH 49:14 NIV

# When God Seems Absent

Sometimes God allows a period of pain and hardship in our lives, a long space where we start to wonder if our walk with God has been just a figment of our imaginations. We begin to doubt His existence—or if we still believe in God, we wonder if He really loves us after all. He seems so far removed from our lives. We can't feel His presence. We can't see His hand at work in our lives.

Sometimes, to add insult to injury, we even beat ourselves up for feeling this way. As women, we're good at blaming ourselves! It must be our fault if we can't feel God, we tell ourselves. If we were more spiritual, more disciplined, better in some way. . .

But even Jesus experienced these same feelings. On the cross, He asked His Father, "My God, my God, why have you abandoned me?" (Matthew 27:46 NLT). Jesus understands our feelings—and He never condemns us for feeling them.

And God answers our fears with these words: "Can a mother forget the baby at her breast. . . ? Though she may forget, I will not forget you!" (Isaiah 49:15 NIV). Then He adds, "See, I have written your name on the palms of my hands" (49:16 NLT).

These are wonderful, human images of God's love for us. If you've been a nursing mother, you know it's impossible to forget your baby; even if your mind and heart could somehow forget, your very body would remind you, so close is the bond you share with your baby. And as for your name written on God's hand—think about when you were a teenage girl: did you ever write the name of the boy you liked on your hand? His name on your skin somehow tied you together.

The God who created the universe loves us like *that*! Believe in His love. Don't worry if you can't *feel* it. Just trust.

And one day, as surely as spring comes after winter, you will once more feel His presence at your side—and you will know then that His strength and His love were always with you, even when you couldn't feel Him there. He will never, ever abandon you.

*Start by doing what's necessary,
then what's possible, and suddenly
you are doing the impossible.*

FRANCIS OF ASSISI

*If winter comes, can spring be far behind?*

PERCY BYSSHE SHELLEY

*The will to persevere is often the difference
between failure and success.*

DAVID SARNOFF

Thank You, God, for loving me.
When life is hard, I'll trust in You.
I know You'll never desert me. I know
Your faithfulness will never end. Amen.

*I am not afraid of storms for I
am learning how to sail my ship.*

LOUISA MAY ALCOTT


*Day follows night. . .flood comes after ebb. . .
spring and summer succeed winter. . . . Hope
thou then! Hope thou ever! God fails thee not.*

CHARLES H. SPURGEON


*Let us learn to cast our hearts into God.*

BERNARD OF CLAIRVAUX

Here, Lord—catch! I'm throwing my heart at You. Don't drop it, please. I'm so tired of trying to carry it on my own. You carry it for me instead. I'm counting on You. Amen.

# The Power
# of Prayer

*"If you seek him, you will find him."*

1 Chronicles 28:9 NLT

# Seeking God in Prayer

The Bible doesn't tell us that we have to pray in a certain way in order to find God. It doesn't teach that we have to follow an elaborate prayer discipline or practice certain techniques. That's not to say that certain disciplines can't be helpful to our spiritual lives, but when it comes right down to it, the Bible makes clear that prayer is very simple. All we have to do is look for God—and whether we can sense His presence with us or not, there He is! It's the very act of turning toward God, the opening ourselves to His potential and power, that is the truest, most basic form of prayer.

Prayer is as simple as the moment when we cry, "Help!" It is the acknowledgment that our own strength is not enough, that we're willing to let go of our own control of our lives and trust in God. Sometimes we may express our prayers in words, sometimes in song. We may be on our knees or facedown on our beds. But God hears us just as well if we're driving in our cars, sitting at our computers, or in the midst of a conversation with a friend.

"Let us come boldly to the throne of our gracious God," advises the writer of Hebrews. "There we will receive his mercy, and we will find grace to help us when we need it" (4:16

NLT). God promises that if we seek Him, we will find Him. He doesn't need a bell or a special signal to bring His attention to us. He's always there, ready to listen, ready to help. All we have to do is turn toward Him.

*Never wait for fitter time or place to talk to Him*
*. . . . He will listen as you walk.*

GEORGE MACDONALD

*The spirit of prayer is a pressing forth of*
*the soul out of this earthly life, it is a stretching*
*with all its desire after the life of God, it is a*
*leaving, as far as it can, all its own spirit, to*
*receive a spirit from above, to be one life,*
*one love, one spirit with Christ in God.*

WILLIAM LAW

*Prayer is as simple as opening our hearts to God,*
*moment by moment, asking God to*
*share every detail of our lives.*

AMY WESTCOTT

*Is anyone among you in trouble? Let them pray.
Is anyone happy? Let them sing songs of praise.
Is anyone among you sick? Let them call the
elders of the church to pray over them and anoint
them with oil in the name of the Lord. And the
prayer offered in faith will make the sick person
well; the Lord will raise them up. If they have
sinned, they will be forgiven. Therefore confess
your sins to each other and pray for each other so
that you may be healed. The prayer of a righteous
person is powerful and effective.*

JAMES 5:13–16 NIV

*Do not be anxious about anything,*
*but in every situation, by prayer and petition,*
*with thanksgiving, present your requests to God.*

PHILIPPIANS 4:6 NIV

# The Habit of Prayer

All of us fear bad news. We dread the sound of the phone ringing in the middle of the night. We may tense up when we hear an ambulance's siren. We worry for our loved ones—and when we do, our hearts pound, and adrenaline flows through our bodies. As women, we can't seem to control those natural reactions. We're just made that way.

But the psalmist tells us that the secret to life's bad news is a steadfast and secure heart (112:7–8 NIV). God can keep our hearts and minds from being washed away in a tide of fear and adrenaline. Prayer is the anchor that can hold us steady, tying us to the God who is unshakable. Our hearts become "steadfast" when we make a habit of turning immediately to God, whenever we feel the slightest nibble of anxiety.

Author Darlene Sala writes, "Bad news is like a storm that rises quickly on the ocean of our lives and would sink our ship if we didn't do something quickly. When the storm comes, we need a harbor where we can drop anchor. 'I would hurry to my place of shelter, far from the tempest and storm,' says the psalmist (55:8 NIV). . .when bad news comes, God is a strong harbor where you can put down the anchor of your heart."

When you fear bad news, don't waste time worrying, letting your fear build up in your heart, mind, and body. Instead, make prayer your constant habit. Keep the anchor of your life safe and secure in God's harbor.

Lord, when bad news comes, remind me to turn to You before I do anything else. I know that when my heart is close to Yours, I will be better able to deal with whatever comes next. Amen.

*Because of our faith, Christ has brought us into this place of undeserved privilege where we now stand, and we confidently and joyfully look forward to sharing God's glory.*

ROMANS 5:2 NLT

*Pray in the Spirit at all times and on every occasion. Stay alert and be persistent in your prayers for all believers everywhere.*

EPHESIANS 6:18 NLT

*Be alert and of sober mind so that you may pray.*

# The Discipline of Prayer

The apostle Peter knew all too well that our selfish fears can come between God and us. After all, he was the one who denied his closest Friend on the night before His death! That's why Peter advises us to be "alert and of sober mind." He knows how easily we're distracted. He knows that when we let our selfish concerns become uppermost in our minds, we lose our ability to communicate with God.

Prayer isn't complicated—but we all too easily forget to do it! We're so busy, running errands, driving here and there, checking our e-mail, making phone calls, multitasking. We feel the constant pressure to somehow keep up with careers and housework, not to mention the demands of family, friends, and community. It's just so hard to make time for prayer!

But Martin Luther reminds us, "I have so many things to do today, I dare not ignore my time with God." And if we follow Peter's advice, we'll clear our minds so we can focus on God.

It's not that God needs us to set aside a special time and place in order for Him to be present with us. God is perfectly capable of hearing us while we sit at our desks, talk on the phone, or drive our cars. And we should turn our hearts to Him in the midst of all our other activities. But *we* need special times and places in order to make a space to focus our thoughts on Him. Without that, it's harder for us to hear God's voice.

Making that time and place requires self-control; it means saying no to other demands so that we can say yes to prayer. It means disciplining our unruly minds to sit quiet, waiting, empty of self—so that God can speak to our hearts.

*No matter how much we talk about prayer or read about prayer or even practice prayer, we don't really understand what it is. How can we possibly understand the reality of speaking intimately with the Creator of the universe?*

AMY WESTCOTT

*A conversation between two friends can be eloquent and fluent—but as equally meaningful a conversation can take place when two friends walk in silence together, exchanging only a word now and then to express the fullness of their hearts. It is the same with prayer: sometimes we will pour out our hearts to God in a stream of words—and sometimes we will simply walk in His presence, knowing He is there with us each step of the way.*

ALFRED DALTON

Clear my thoughts, Lord, so I can focus on You. Be present with me; be my most intimate Friend. Let me never forget to turn to You in prayer. Amen.

# A Personal Savior

*I trust in your unfailing love;*
*my heart rejoices in your salvation.*

PSALM 13:5 NIV

# Saving Love

All of us need love. And all of us, at one time or another, feel unloved. Deep in our hearts, we don't believe we even deserve to be loved.

God understands those feelings. And He longs to convince us that at the deepest, most intimate level of our beings, we are truly loved. The Bible repeats this message of love over and over—and yet we hesitate to grab hold of this reality.

Author James Bryan Smith paraphrases some of the love letters written in the Bible this way:

*I have called you by name, from the very beginning.*

   *You are mine and I am yours.*

   *You are my Beloved, on you my favor rests.*

   *I have molded you from the depths of the earth and knitted you together in your mother's womb.*

   *I have carved you in the palms of my hands and hidden you in the shadow of my embrace. . . .*

   *I never expected you would be perfect.*

   *I love you. I love you. I love you.*

   *Nothing will ever change that.*

Love is the reason Jesus came to earth.

Love was the message He brought to us from God. Not a generic, all-purpose sort of love, either, but a unique love for each one of us, specific to our own hearts. We are each called by name, saved by love.

His love is written in your very being. And you see His love everywhere you look, for that is what holds the world together.

*Our Lord has written the promise of
the resurrection, not in books alone,
but in every leaf in springtime.*

MARTIN LUTHER


*The Bible tells us that Jesus is the One who
"holds all things together." We see His
saving grace everywhere we turn.*

ANNE WILMOT


*The world is not the cold, indifferent place it often
seems, nor it is the mechanical machine scientists
have sometimes described. Ancient humans knew
the world was a living, breathing thing—and
as Christians, we need to cultivate a vision
that perceives our Savior's image in earth and
water, in beast and tree, in stars and sunshine,
and even in city streets and human faces.*

RIVAH BROWN

Jesus answered, "I am the way and the truth and the life. No one comes to the Father except through me."

JOHN 14:6 NIV

Jesus is " 'the stone you builders rejected, which has become the cornerstone.' Salvation is found in no one else."

ACTS 4:11–12 NIV

"My dear Martha, you are worried and upset over all these details! There is only one thing worth being concerned about. Mary has discovered it, and it will not be taken away from her."

LUKE 10:41–42 NLT

# "Martha" and "Mary" Prayers

Martha seems to have gotten the short end of the stick sometimes. The poor woman, she was rushing around taking care of all the practical details involved with having Jesus as a guest in her home—and then He scolded her for not being more like her sister, who was just sitting at His feet, doing nothing. We can imagine Martha giving a long-suffering sigh, thinking to herself, *Well, I'd like to know who would mash the potatoes and set the table if I was sitting in here next to Mary.*

If we're honest, most of us relate to Martha. We scurry through our lives, scolding our kids and spouses to hurry up, trying to get everything done, feeling impatient with anything that gets in our way. Our to-do lists are just so long!

We may make sure to put prayer on that long list of tasks to be checked off, but when we sit down to pray, we often still have a "Martha" attitude. We briskly work our way through our prayer requests: *Dear Lord, please do this and please do that.* Without realizing what we're doing, we may even think of the Lord as one more person we have to nudge along, lest He forget to accomplish all that needs to be done.

God probably just smiles at us patiently. He waits for us to finally let all the busyness go so that we can, like Mary, simply sit in His presence. He wants our prayers to come from a "Mary" heart, one that's willing to listen, one that's willing to do absolutely nothing so that God can speak.

We all get so upset about the details. But when we let them all drop into God's hands, we can finally relax. We can come to Jesus in love and trust, as Mary did.

Dear Jesus, give me a Mary heart. When I get so busy that I'm all filled up with Martha, quiet my mind. Slow me down. Let me hear Your voice calling me to come sit down beside You and rest. Amen.

*For you know the grace of our Lord Jesus Christ,*
*that though he was rich, yet for your sake*
*he became poor, so that you through his*
*poverty might become rich.*

2 CORINTHIANS 8:9 NIV

*And the Word was made flesh, and dwelt*
*among us, (and we beheld his glory, the glory*
*as of the only begotten of the Father,)*
*full of grace and truth.*

JOHN 1:14 KJV

*Christ died once for all time as a sacrifice to take*
*away the sins of many people. He will come again,*
*not to deal with our sins, but to bring salvation to*
*all who are eagerly waiting for him.*

HEBREWS 9:28 NLT

*So the Word became human and made his home among us.*
*He was full of unfailing love and faithfulness.*
*And we have seen his glory.*

JOHN 1:14 NLT

# Christmas All Year Round

At Christmastime, more than any other, we remember that Jesus came to this world. Everywhere we turn, glowing lights and softly playing carols remind us of His birth. But our world often acts as though the Christmas story were a pretty fairy tale, a sentimental scene edged with sweet-faced angels, fluffy white sheep, and yellow stars, something to be trotted out once a year and then stored away till next December along with all the decorations.

We forget that Jesus' birth was no Disney movie. This is the story that changed the world forever. The King of creation came to live in the midst of poverty and dirt and pain. . . and even death. By doing so, He conquered death and changed the world forever. What's more, He changed *us* forever. He is the world's Savior—and He is each of ours, individually.

He didn't stop being the King when He became a Child. His innocence triumphed over all earth's tragedy. Sometimes it may seem as though the forces of evil are winning. But in reality, the Christmas Child is always on His throne—and His saving grace is always working. His story has power for us all year long, in March and July and October, as much as in December!

The magi, those three kings from the East, were wise enough to set aside their own worldly power and position. Instead, they yielded their lives to the guidance of a star— and when they found the Child, they bowed down and offered Him their treasures. May we all be wise enough to do the same, all year round!

*The Word of God, Jesus Christ, on account of His great love for mankind, became what we are in order to make us what He is Himself.*

BERNARD OF CLAIRVAUX


*Before the world was ever created, Jesus was my Savior. He stands outside time, and so forever and eternity, His identity is knit into my own. I would not exist without Him, for His saving grace is in every cell of my body.*

ANNE WILMOT


*Jesus knocks at the door of our hearts, and when we open, He fill us with His joy.*

CORRIE TEN BOOM

$\mathcal{L}$ord Jesus, I open myself to You. Live within me. Make Yourself at home in my heart. Thank You for saving me, now and forever. Amen.

# Scripture Index

## Old Testament

# NEW TESTAMENT